CRITICAL ACCLAIM

Paul Edward Costa is a poet-explorer of the inner life as we all live it, as we recognize it in our most complete moments. He's one of those explorers with a wonderful gift for telling the tale and describing the places of his far travels in direct language that conveys wonders of sensitive intuition. Sample for yourself the depth and energy of just the first three poems of the book and you'll be hooked. You'll see why, as the book progresses, the Costa-poet's "mind stripped bare" understands the contemporary self as an ever-healing, ever-searching, never finished "half- human creature thing." With invigorating psychological honesty and realism, *Some Half-Human Creature Thing* depicts his and our arrival "floating in suspension, far above the world" at "an uncertain place only accessible by…a straight road to a point of dissolution."

—A.F. Moritz
Former Toronto Poet Laureate and author
of *Great Silent Ballad: Poems*

Paul Edward Costa's poetry is tinged with haunting. Whether in "the dark matter lurking in this dimension," along a woods trail in Mississauga, or "abstract monstrosities," his work reflects on fear and uncertainty in a tumultuous world. But within this darkness, Costa brings humour into his musings, "like if the language of Babel had been destroyed / by a hallucinogenic fungus / instead of a furious god." Prepare to be surprised by the turns in Costa's imagery, a world where "steampunk sunflowers" bloom and "sentinels…seek and destroy."

—Manahil Bandukwala
Author of *Monument and Heliotropia*

Paul Edward Costa's poetry is one of engagement. Engagement with the self, and engagement with whatever it is that you want to call what we've made of our miserable and exquisite world. As Mississauga poet laureate, he did not shy away from speaking truth to power, as in "State-Sponsored Elegy", which deals frankly with Death By Cop. He is also concerned about where society is headed, and predicts we will become criminals because soon only outlaws will enjoy face-to-face human interaction. Costa's is a world where hauling existential dread is an athletic event;

where unexpected beauty – such as that of satellite dishes, which are nothing less than steampunk sunflowers – will save us; and where a single punctuation mark can make all the difference in how we relate to ourselves: for what a journey there is to go from asking ourselves "Why am I like this?" to "Why, am I like this?"

—Richard-Yves Sitoski
Former Owen Sound Poet Laureate
and author of *Wait, What?*

Paul Edward Costa's *Some Half-Human Creature Thing* is a collection of poetry full of contradictions. It is intimate while evoking a sense of remoteness. It is unadorned in style, yet the byroads in its lines are labyrinthine. Altogether, *Some Half-Human Creature Thing* is an odyssey that takes the reader from the heart of inner turmoil to fantastical and experimental landscapes, to the open and ever-grown arms of suburban Mississauga streets. All the while, one gets the sense that the author is sitting right there with them, quiet in the comfortable silence of the familiar.

—Rocco De Giacomo, author of *Casting Out*

SOME HALF-HUMAN CREATURE THING

SOME HALF-HUMAN CREATURE THING

Paul Edward Costa

Library and Archives Canada Cataloguing in Publication

Title: Some half-human creature thing / poetry by Paul Edward Costa.

Names: Costa, Paul Edward, 1989- author.

Identifiers: Canadiana (print) 20240474031
Canadiana (ebook) 20240478649

ISBN 9781771617840 (softcover) | ISBN 9781771617864 (EPUB)
ISBN 9781771617857 (PDF) | ISBN 9781771617871 (Kindle)

Subjects: LCGFT: Poetry.

Classification: LCC PS8605.O872726 S66 2024
DDC C811/.6—dc23

Published by Mosaic Press, Oakville, Ontario, Canada, 2025.
MOSAIC PRESS, Publishers
www.Mosaic-Press.com

Cover Design: Rahim Piracha

Printed and bound in Canada.

Funded by the Government of Canada
Financé par le gouvernement du Canada

MOSAIC PRESS
1252 Speers Road, Units 1 & 2, Oakville, Ontario, L6L 2X4 (905) 825-2130
info@mosaic-press.com • www.mosaic-press.com

To my family—my father, Manuel; my mother, Ingrid; my sister, Caroline; and my brother, Kevin. With deep gratitude to my grandparents, whose journey from Portugal, Slovakia, and Germany brought us to Canada.

ALSO BY PAUL EDWARD COSTA

GOD DAMNED AVALON (2021)

THE LONG TRAIN OF CHAOS (2019)

TABLE OF CONTENTS

MISSISSAUGA POET LAUREATE POEMS

THE NERVOUSNESS MANIFESTO

A warm welcome
makes anxious thoughts
paint on a moustache
then walk back and forth
while waving a cigar
saying there must be a serious flaw
in any club that would have me as a member,

insisting only a broken lens
could view the fractured reality
of whatever-the-hell-it-is I think I am
in a positive configuration,

before proposing isolation
as a way of sparing the normal world
some kind of damaging exposure
to the dark matter lurking in this dimension

until they exit stage left
and leave me alone to make a decision
since anxious thoughts
only ever ask vague questions
then sit back and watch
from front row seats
while frozen panic sets in.

LIKE TEARS IN ICE

It is quite an experience
to put your heart
between
a pair of hands
praying through pain
        near the arrival
        of their agony's anniversary
while also trying
to master stillness
in an unhinged corridor
      under a shooting star
that might fly by its enduring chaos
 or maybe make impact
    with a frenetic reality
          finally able to stand still.

MEET THE MEMORIZED CITY

The quiet is different downtown
                after buildings drain
            daytime sounds
into subways:
a creeping dread without cause,
in this context
like a cold nausea coming on.

How? Driving intervals of unlit roads
didn't bring this same
subterranean sadness,
this sick fear
near glass foyers
and terrace gardens looking haunted
without the sun sealed in reflections
of adjacent windows.

I couldn't visit
the city after nightfall for years
until a song's
frozen vocals and keyboard tones
let me equalise my internal state
with so much frigid
external space;
it's a relief I keep trying to explain
                                        or recreate.

PSYCHO-LYCANTHROPY

Believing my body is nothing
but bones wrapped in flesh
made it all the more frightening
when the personality
        of a person I thought I knew
            changed like a season setting in overnight,
                like the vessel I recognized
                became a disguise,
bringing brain freeze
to my engine
seizing up
because anything
could hide behind the persona
I've granted access to my thoughts,
a wheel of fortune spinning through
the whole spectrum of a human heart,
not landing on kindness
            or compassion
but a black hole of hate warping the mind
come close to mine,
a sun collapsing into cruelty
        until my shifting gears
        lift survival
above civility,
appeasement,
and a programmed need to be polite,
        pushing me away from a place
            even light can't escape
            while always obscuring
            the bright shapes of other stars.

WHERE NO SUNS SHINE

Some ideas or feelings
seem completely beyond articulation:
like a black hole,
you have to infer what's there,
when nothing is visible
by way of what's arranged on the fringes,
which is likely why
we use words to work out
what's generated by the jellified
electrical storms we carry in bone cases
                                        on our shoulders
and use examples in the hope
that those images
make other sets of synapses
crackle in the same way,

but I've never been able to make anyone else get
the same sensation of beauty and wonder
I feel when I see
a massive satellite array of antennae on a field,
                                colossal, concave dishes
                                synchronised and aimed at the purpose
                                                    of investigating heaven
while simultaneously looking
like a pristine bed of steampunk sunflowers
cultivated by an iron giant.

Friends who've known me well have never understood
and maybe I don't either,
with the words I use to describe that image
being as close as I can get
        to the deep experience
                around which they orbit.

SPEAK FRIEND AND ENTER

Writing is hard.
For example, it's taken me
                    two years
to learn how to add
the comma
and italics
that change the question
          "Why am I like this?"
to the realisation
of asking myself
          "Why, am *I* like this?"
in acceptance
of my mirror image with a mind of its own,
the reflection I'm seeing
          for the first time.

ICONOCLAST DECORATING LTD.

I just can't bring myself
  to chisel my history into the walls around me
because I'm worried
I'll experience a storm others never see,
                    some kind of subjective anomaly,
that'll leave my mind on mute
        while worshipping familiar carvings
that seem to have transcended the fragile accountability
of my flesh and bones
with lines etched into rock,
                              only two levels
stone that's broken
                         and stone that's not
as fifty-two layers of my personality
              shuffle over another truth
that alone and unmoored,
I'm afraid,
     afraid I'll forget myself
     and see no choice
but to try and be the ideal being on the walls
each day
         and every night
         until I start believing that I am the myth of a projected,
                                                    partial persona.

TAKE A BALLOON AND GO SAILING

There's a subtle art to splitting yourself in half
and projecting your spirit onto a far-off ridge
or somewhere up into stratospheric clouds
where it can always analyse extra footprints
around the spots where you stumbled,
where it can always measure your wavering walk
against paths disappearing straight into sinkholes ahead,
and you shouldn't overfeed your astral projection
or let it be fooled by feeling like a god
floating in the sky;
if it gets too powerful
and its cravings too large,
it'll tear through your memories
in a search for spiritual sustenance,
digging further
and further back
because your body's been stumbling
over barren plains in a trance
between dirt hills and bare trees,
beneath power lines like horizontal blinds,
that are stretched across the sun.

CHICKEN LITTLE IN THE STYLE OF A 1970s CONSPIRACY THRILLER

You'll know heaven is about to fall
        when a few angels plunge through the sky,
thrown down
for noticing corrosion on the golden gates
        and cracks growing in heavenly spheres.
The only way of avoiding their impact
                is by living in spots
over which they never watched
while the only way of knowing
when a sinkhole might consume the ground beneath your feet
        is to interview broken celestial bodies
in deep craters,
scribble their prophecies onto scrolls
instead of into brittle stone,
and hope you don't get thrown into a bottomless pit
when you bring those words to your world.

I NEVER SAID THANK YOU

If broken eggshells could speak,
they may forgive us
for the sacrifice we ask
while suggesting that we might
at least,
address them directly
and say a quick prayer
of apologetic acknowledgement
before tearing a few apart
or boiling their soft innards
into hardened states of devilry
then, ideally,
lay their corpses down
in organic fields of decay
so that they might, at least
give some strength
back to life with their flesh.

THE FUNCTION OF COLD JESTERS

Historians chronicling the utopia usually
leave out any mention of a Cold Jester,

not Court Jester,
one who'd come in through crisply even snow,

or a purveyor of temperature trick-turns either,
defecating infinite sunshine.

Their role's responsibility rose out of being
lone, dense, counterpoints to their country's character,

outside its warmth but with a clear perspective cutting
through waves of abstract issues coming down

Why does the new bakery make small loaves quick to mould?
Why don't they reach out if touched by misfortune?

The cause lies in corners utopians can't see
so Cold Jesters unveil their truth after chewing bitter leaves:

how it's cheaper to make them tiny with poor quality wheat
when cost takes quality's place of priority

while utopic councillors collapse
under the
weight of nauseous migraines
during this cynical blizzard, this quick glimpse

into their out-of-sight nightmare dimension
and that's when Cold Jesters serve a second function

as harlequin assassins so employed because
it was decided those who see an issue should face it

and in such a violent, final capacity because
hell has no fury like a prideful fear of imperfection

making Cold Jesters dispose of the derangements they perceive
until they're so thoroughly stained

that the utopia they serve has no place for them
on the flawless, hyperbolic tapestry

so retirement means a solitary exile to remote regions
where many satisfy their natural conditioning

for stoic, observational clarity
by taking up various avenues of study

like history as seen by exiled eyes
or the deep, expanding meditation of astronomy.

TWISTED METAL SCHOOL BUS

You can imagine
why they pulled
    that particular episode
    of children's programming from the airwaves
where a broken soul
on a frayed neuron tether
hijacks the magic school bus,
commanding it to *Drive!*
or shrink!
or whatever…
into an acquaintance's brain
so that they might understand how someone close
can hear a picture of pain
            painted by vocal chords
and have their first instinct be
to openly state
                not sympathy,
but how glad they are
that they're not the one
    confined in the speaker's mental cell.

TWENTY-THREE HOUR LOCKDOWN

The best prison cell
doesn't need steel bars
or layers of physical confinement:
all it needs is a vestibule
and two unlocked doors,
    one holding a lens
        amplifying the length
        of roads winding behind you,
    one hiding the promise
        of wonders soon to come through,
        and the assurance
            that what you anticipate
              is nearly within view,
bolstered by a fear of backtracking
and recalculating
  a route to lesser treasures
    than what you think will appear.

THE HATE PARADE

The only ones watching the parade
are those wishing to join
processions of ritual purpose
possessed by ecstatic expressions.

Observers don't rush the floats
in mobs spoiling a desirable display
whose emergence and disappearance
no one sees
while too awestruck to move
and it's a good thing they are;
anyone cursed with too clear,
                                        too direct
                                        trains of thought
finds the place from where the cavalcade comes
                                   and where it eventually goes,
showing why jubilations
                                   of exaltation seize those in it
when they can come out
                                   to feel the sun for a few hours,
only beset by blessed celebrations,
a relief to all except the few
tormented by being
so tantalisingly close to escape,
and thwarted
by how crowds viciously kills
anyone who gets off
for *acts of ingratitude.*
Those who can't fake enough joy
wear mascot suits of another's flesh
with permanently smiling
                                        mouths stitched up

as city guards stay far back and watch
in fear of what those too jaded
to follow the parade might find
if they unanchor their attention
from a perpetually moving spectacle
then wander off,
unchecked and self-possessed.

CRIMINOLOGICAL

Eventually
the main reason people turn to crime
as a way of life
won't be financial opportunity,
          for the most part,
the anxious thrill
          of evading capture,
or the freedom in living past the rules
                              of normal society;
the main thing
               that'll make people
               commit to criminal groups
               will be a longing for the privacy
                                        and bonding
only available
     while working in secret,
the way that lifestyle
     forces every interaction
 under the radar
into the realm
     of in-person meetings,
        face-to-face
in parks, parking lots
or the droning noise of a laundromat,
like mafia movies
with a deeper sense of community
than what's found in legally omniscient
telecommunications
as traceable as they are accessible,
unlimited, though rooted in cold distance,
and with an immaterial quality both freeing
and formless in equal measure.

POST-SECONDARY STRESS DISORDER: KNOW THE SYMPTOMS

I opened a message
autocorrected to proclaim
only these cryptic words:

Rock. Thank you.

instead of the intended text,
and I've obsessed for years now
over whether or not
the sender ever meditated on its meaning
as I did...and still do,
though I admit
I lack the language courses needed
to fully grasp
and appreciate its message
filled either with heavy wisdom
as I so desperately hope,
or only the harsh, pixelated headache
of progress and communication randomly collapsing
as I so desperately fear,
like if the language of Babel had been destroyed
by a hallucinogenic fungus
instead of a furious god.

I WAS BUT THE LEARNER

Raised to follow this
aged art your master barely
endures in secret:
more sacrifice than student
before a forced unlearning.

You'll find an empty
scholar's lounge when you arrive;
they saw what draws near.

So now
you'll run
and then
convince
yourself
this was
your goal
with no atonement from
proponents of the futile path.

FUTILITY IS THE KEY

A blue light bus
through paved deserts to future voices e
choing in stone chambers,

a blurred shriek of contradictions
amid cackling implosions
from a village on the edge of shadows,

their shepherds are impatient
and the road to perdition is plagued
by construction delays.

I've heard prayers
to fairy folk for relief
or to butterflies in a stone garden

but enduring sanctuary, for now
is a small screen at midnight,
scripted laughter,
and commercials from an emerald Eden
two hours north of here.

IT RAINS A LOT IN THE FIFTH DIMENSION

Nothing makes you feel lost
                    in Slaughterhouse-Five's unstuck time
like telling tales of years you lived
    to ears hearing them
    as anecdotes of an ancient age.
Reflecting is one thing;
this is leaping through a continuum,
not dwelling or remembering too long
if it's all in the present
for a psyche sliding back
into days of future past
when sentinels sent to seek and destroy
close in,
adapting to their target;
        for me they're judges accepting
        every old crime as a clear precedent
        for predicting what's to come,
until I fear any shadows on the wall I face
and hear gavels hammering the point of free will
into a gravel road
unless I'm able to grab hold of the cable pulling me
through bygone storms to barren futures
and can swing it in three hundred and fifty-eight more directions
                    than a grandfather clock's binary pendulum.

WE SHALL MEDITATE ON THE BEACHES

Our lives become the constant roar of time
crashing in waves over the shoreline
until we listen
to the moon's lunar melody
pulling water onto crumbling continents
with tides like looming realities,
each one more terrifying in its approach
than after washing over us,
while levelling sandcastles
and raising shipwrecks
alongside a swelling mass of lost artefacts
reasserting their long presence
and revealing a truth beneath the dunes
in every relic
able to relate the real meaning
of old, pastime proverbs
repurposed
by the ruling powers of our present.

DEFENDER OF THE ABSURD

How stubborn was he?
Well,
he had the kind of hell-bent mind
that made him travel
backwards through time,
breaking swords before
pushing feathered quills
or calligraphy pens
into the corpses
of dead knights and samurai
desperately justifying an idiom
and the comforting illusion
that platitude prayers
come from a place of proven,
earthen wisdom.

A MYTHIC GREEK TORMENT

They said
wear a gas mask
        because everyone inside
        exhales nerve gas
        instead of carbon dioxide,
leaving lingering pools
of a substance that causes seizures when pins fall on stone,
that makes you feel worthy of eternal silence,
                        that causes paralysis in the age of the dance,
                        that sneaks up
                        and slits the throat of father time
                        in front of your passive eyes.
They said
wear a gas mask
because, for them,
        never exhaling poison
meant never inhaling air,
forcing visitors to filter the oxygen
no one purifies, essentially
    using a thousand bloody bandages
    instead of cauterising a wound
    as a lethal fog fills the halls
and the only affection
is a sterile kiss between two gas mask filters
                            as they gently touch
                                    then come apart.

MADMAN ABOVE THE CITY

Somehow
this conqueror
still needs to feel infusions of power
from a desperate populace crawling to his feet
as he summons subjects
just to call upon his judgement

but before he can change this conversation
let me reveal
how our mad titan doesn't bring direct destruction:

he contents himself with selecting
what he wants to survive while ignoring
carved rock diverging from one vision,
never smashing statues
while preferring to polish only a pretty few,
like a posh prince or a ship of dreams
as he lets decay lay waste to the rest
so he can't be accused of taking his hammer
to a museum's sculptures
with no stone dust on his pants or shirt…
in fact,
his hands have never borne a speck of dirt;
how else can he always mistake his reflection
for visions of a sun so gloriously risen?

THE CHRONOS COOKBOOK

The most effective method
of massacring Mount Olympus
is to simply
walk through its marble pillars
before driving a gardening spade,
                                        sewing needle,
                                or other domestic tool
between the ribs of its denizens.

The reason why
lies in how
they won't realise you're wielding a weapon.
In fact,
they won't know what you're holding,
thinking it just
                some weird little sculpture they've never seen
from their mountain's towering perch
filled only with gleaming armour,
                and glittering halberds,
                by platinum pens
under disintegrating paper decrees
alongside stone monuments to themselves
they like better than the real-time terror
                                        of a reflection.

ABOVE THE ARENA

Only deities
history didn't push over the world's edge
can praise what they see as
            Medusa's poetic end,
recounting

the perfectly preserved,
   romantic eternity of her fate
   in a rock shaped
      like her legacy

with soft lips,
vocal chords still vibrating,
and all sense of irony
      stripped away.

THE UNHOLY MOUNTAIN

The pilgrims on the road aren't stooped low as they walk because of a force or energy bearing on their shoulders as they look down instead of at the destination they seek.

They're walking off-balance and hunched over because of past trauma and future fear: the oppressive amount of distance they've had to cover mixed with a taunting splendour in the palace far ahead made a mental weight

so heavy that strongman competitions will one day have a category for pulling the physical mass of a passenger plane while bearing similarly heavy, existential emotions.

Those looking down while on the road see a shadow of the palace they approach and can't be convinced by forward scouts that it's a mountain.

How can it be that if it produces light and ejects smoke like it does, as only a space inhabited by humans does?

Because smoke rises from the void that mountain tries to hide and lightning strikes hit deposits of ore unearthed inside.

But with so few praying to the wind anymore there haven't been gusts that could push the storm along or disperse the dark clouds coming up,

concealing a clear perspective of the land from the mountain and obscuring a view of it from those who beheld its form.

Witnesses who could stop this lurching drama only watched, insisting that it wasn't their place to reveal truth to the pilgrims

although anyone who couldn't cut themselves off from seeing cause and effect knew that the collision of the enshrouded mountain and deceived holy travellers would be far more catastrophic than a few dashed hopes.

They watched with the rapt anticipation of deep satisfaction felt by those seeing two determined motions push past physical laws to a destructive catharsis only the watcher can experience.

But no such satisfied interlocking of chaos took place because the pilgrims resisting long depression's gravity and the mountain clouded by smoke with electricity inside never met.

The nature of each would never permit a combination of these elements to exist with any level of stability or longevity.

The mountain dug deeper into itself and prayed harder to thunderous conduction as it saw, through its dark cloud veil, satanic shadows come closer en mass after emerging from the earth

and bent-over pilgrims became so enamoured with the grand palace they perceived that they pinned every hope on it and brushed off immediate problems as things that will certainly be made right after arriving at their destination,

so they crumpled into the depths within themselves when their dream could no longer override psychological and biological necessities

as the unholy mountain collapsed into caverns inside itself that it widened while looking for any solution other than actual clarity.

THE EXILE'S EPIPHANY

Far away from a King
the kingdom forgot how to question
outlaws on a long walk
accept that every charlatan needs a legion
                    whose devotion is a token
                              for private moments
when illusions lift and reveal
a life of inertia,
              sold instead
              as tragically thwarted dreams,
                   scenes of two-faced Janus
                   showing one good side
as accusations of deceit collide
with the myth of a noble sacrifice
where carrying a cross
isn't the same without a crowd
        and Mary Magdalene
                crying for Gnostic gods
                while imposter syndrome grows
into a religious revival,
            praising a preacher
making high jumps over low bars
from the flock's perspective
in a Waco state of mind,
burning for the oceanic feeling
of coming together to love their master,
a persona thoughts won't forget
                 until they're reduced to see-through,
                                                  skeletal words
and are cast into a page's white abyss
                                                      like this.

AT THE LIMITS OF GUIDANCE

With all due gratitude,
to you, my guide,
for explaining this road,

your having
come back to do so
means you can't again know

how it is
to behold
the shadow gate's debut

and my outburst
came from how
I expected you to.

Now, somewhat settled
I'll only say,
maybe more for me than you,

how my fear wasn't borne
of hellish visions
meaning annihilation;

my terror came
from hallucinations of feeling
like I'm being stretched

over fire forever
in caverns
never devoid of oxygen.

BEHOLD THE BEASTS

Beware the son,
the father,
and the fucked up ghost
using confusion over which came first,
if any did,
to absolve themselves of responsibilities,
pretending their toxic trinity
is a whole society
where voices of reason and empathy
are too low to hear
like screaming from anyone wounded
by the perpetual dance
of their spinning triangle's
sharpened points.

BED, BATH, & WAY BELOW

What if I say
        every pillow
        into which
        you let you a stifled scream
        stores traces of that venom
        after each
        primal utterance?
And then describe
        how they,
        during the dead of night
        pass through portals
in a sofa's deep abyss
to that common subworld
where they conduct their congress
for hate-saturated cushions,
externalising articulations
of what they hold inside,
exchanges whose by-products include
tough formations
mistaken for popcorn,
pressure-formed coinage
and gritty, anonymous bits
      of residual bile,
background radiation
from big bangs
deep beneath our comfort,
a vile presence

we can only blame on flatulence
for so long
before someone
or something else
gets off the couch
instead of our real selves
the next time we stand up?

What then?
Will that be enough
to acknowledge
the risks of our darkness
where by seeing,
perchance,
we might heal?
Or will we commit
to a wish for protection
so strong
that we ignore our slowly
corrupting reflections?

STRIKE A DEAD SENSATION

A mind builds tolerance
to more than intoxicants,
adjusting for instincts dulled
as well as senses deranged.
Manipulated,
over-leveraged
capacities for guilt bend
                    only so far
before they buckle
and move thereafter
    with immediate, frightening ease,
losing shape while going cold
until they no longer snap into formation
when a beast imitates
      a baby's scream,
unable to distinguish
anymore
between rose-thorns,
and coyote fangs camouflaged
                        at midnight
                        by dirt-stained fur.

GUILTY FEET WITHOUT RHYTHM

More minds imploded before unfolding
and revealing their thoughts, true or not
in the constantly quiet din of Whisper Cells
where interrogators sat far from each subject,

only talking inaudibly among themselves
with no one else about whom they could speak

and those almost imperceptible accusations
kept captives convinced of uncertainty
where perceived defeat eventually
eroded every fortified constitution
cast in concrete.

LAO TZU THROUGH THE STAR GATE

I've nearly forgotten
the design of the gate through which I passed
when I left the western province.
It was once my path's only culmination,
the marker,
the endpoint,
the stark watcher standing at the edge
of my dreams
with folded arms,
daring me to get closer
and touch that goal post,
knowing full well my inability to stop walking,
my addiction to the momentum
of accumulated progress
into barren lands beyond
a tangible silence,
a heavy absence,
a total fear in sweat-soaked palms
and an unanchored mind
that doesn't know
where to settle.
But it's been months, a year, a year and a half
and the gate fades into memory's
overexposed sunset
the farther I push into a place that's broken so many
after five steps
that I've started daring myself, asking just how far I can take this road,
what land lies past the next horizon,
and what unknown state I'll inhabit when I arrive,
if I recognize my arrival.

FIST OF THE THIRD QUARTER MOON

While strapped in
to the passenger side seat
of a four-wheel ATV
        racing over forest roads
and flying through midnight's darkness,
I found that relaxing my iron grip
on the bar attached to the door
took more strength
than making a clenched fist with my damaged hand,
or maybe a different kind,
but the real trick
is learning how to let go
without losing a firm grasp
on why you deserve the experience
                        of being alive.

SWINGING SWORDS LIKE SHINOBI

Training on a frozen lake,
my sword master told me
to never hide the scars he'll make
on my arms and face
or else they'll think this path is easy,
he'd say,
for better or worse,
teaching me not to trust
a warrior who claims they've never been cut,
but that's the boast they like hearing the most
before calling on a body
tattooed with scar tissue
                when a new issue
needs someone who can walk on a razor's edge
                                        or stand near a ledge
without slipping on their sweat,
though someone like that, it's alleged,
can't be allowed
to hold a hallowed relic:
              a ruby heart
        or a sapphire teardrop.
When you stand near real danger,
or wonder,
your rushing blood is all you hear
while you feel a numb absence
                whose presence was never there
in old tales of adventure
so I'm training here
on this frozen lake,
            feeling nothing from my fingers to my feet
                while my mind is clear
and my rushing blood is all I hear.

YOU BECOME SOMETHING ELSE ENTIRELY

Be careful who you praise
for being brave,
because drawing a sword
and facing the cavalry
on foot
can come from conviction,
from loving something greater
than yourself
or it can come
from a reckless disregard for selfhood
born of believing you're beyond salvation
and that the only choice left
is choosing a good place
to crash the smoking, fiery wreckage
of an airship losing altitude
so slowly it's impossible to remember
when the descent began,
keeping hold of the controls
because,
by comparison,
a parachute feels powerless, adrift,
and at the mercy of the wind.

A MAGICIAN'S LIMIT

I can learn every card trick illusion,
              making magic with jokers
              and four suits in transit
              among folds of clothing,
or go one step further
by actually manipulating matter into mutations
until I imitate Dr. Moreau,
and yet,
none of these achievements
will explain
how someone can retcon their past
to pretend lilacs always
   gave them a migraine
as soon as the fear they can't face
says violet leaves
levied every headache humans have had,
        when pulling up floral roots is easier
        than pulling down a fuming factory,
even if purple flowers
were the only relief they felt
                    after clocking out.

THE CTHULHU COMPLEX

Somewhere
a script show scenes
      of people
      sewn into a centipede
while
somewhere else
a psychologist trained
in object relations is crying
like a first-person narrator
   uncovering causeways
   leading all the way to a cosmic nightmare.

STRANGELY DRESSED FOR A HIKE

Strangely dressed for a hike,
he's in his dark suit
while she wears a black dress,
both descending forest paths
to grieve at the river's edge
beneath a concrete bridge
indifferent overhead.
She's holding
white roses to spread
while he emanates
helpless anger
at whatever power
forced this extreme
juxtaposition of aesthetics
into existence

BRIDGE TROLL DREAMS

The Troll burns bridges
      so frequently
      I have to stop and wonder
if they get a buzz from inhaling the fumes
      of their shelter set ablaze overhead,
if they think collecting tolls
from terrified travellers
is too great a responsibility,
or if they simply believe
that pilgrims turn back too easily
      from the rugged paths they pick
      before starting their journey.

THE DAUGHTER OF OCEANUS

Forest,
smother light
and nurture subtle shadows,
keep the bull of Zeus back
halted at your borders
and swans imprisoned
in the sky above your trees
where the Dryad named Leuce rules,
naked and levelled with the leaves,
vicious, elegant, hidden, and readied,
all these things at once,
enabled by her mysticism
to be them everywhere at once,
holding a deer skull up
over her face as a crown
to remain grounded
in the constant violence of reality
while channelling
the white poplar tree
of Hades.

THE RAINS OF AZZIRAD FELL

The rains of Azzirad fell,
making the skin of canyon tribesmen
                    transparent
before they started distrusting
anyone
  hiding the organs keeping them alive.

The rains of Azzirad fell,
making coastal tribesmen deaf
before they started distrusting
anyone
    hearing music in lapping waves,

both canyon and coast
waging perpetual war
        in pursuit of secrets already known
as prisoners of the canyon suffer
                                living dissection
while
prisoners of the coast suffer
                            large bells ringing
                            over their heads until
                            their eardrums shatter and bleed.

I sent orders of peace
        to both chiefs
on papyrus
the rains of Azzirad fell upon
and dissolved,
returning messengers in a daze,
describing it as a place

with muddy fields of emerald grass
where the petrified corpses
  of a thousand fowls
  choke on twisted agony,
  beaks bent and screaming
with wings raised
  in an acceptance of mass death
  or a desperate invocation of the divine:
a last plea for grace
as
the rains of Azzirad fell.

TAPPING A STRAINED MIND FOR SYRUP

No,
you didn't miss
any important information
from a prior conversation;
I'm just
a cacophonic
  symphony
of clashing emotions.

MY MIND STRIPPED BARE BY ITS ABSENCE, UNEVEN

Paul Edward Costa
In an Uncertain Place
Only Accessible by
Taking a Straight Road
to a Point of Dissolution

No truth,
no answer,
explanation,
or closure:

-Learn to write ***S I L E N C E*** slowly in the void.
-Letters become swarming wasps
waging war around your head
in a place
where you're forced to stand still.

a balanced mind on a ping-pong table is a symbol for
repeat this phrase forever
but
a player returning a serve by screaming
has a chance of moving forward

filling empty space and taking its shape so well
the vacuum regains its vacancy
as hollow containers implode.

Fairies rising from fading photos,
show a way inside...

though I've impaled them with pins
like butterflies in a frame;
I don't think the pictures are real anymore
if they ever were
and I don't believe their reality
if I ever did.

The stages of loss become
1. You miss what was there
2. You miss being able
to remember what you saw
0. You feel like nothing ever stood in that spot
0. Even if you know something has

Me [*filled with determination*]: Push through the asteroids and airless distance, past the edge of your universe, to a planet filled with stuffed animals that feel warm to the touch...

Also Me [*fearing vulnerability*]: ...But keep your spacesuit on as you hold them, in case they're animated by lethal radiation...

...now I'm floating in suspension, far above the world...

MISSISSAUGA POET LAUREATE POEMS
(APRIL 2019-NOVEMBER 2021)

FROM ANCIENT VERSE

A baton touches my hand when it swings back and
in an instant
I'm not a solitary runner on a cracked desert;
it dawns on me that I never have been.
I'm linked to a train
reaching from the cool, steady hand
passing this position to mine,
all the way back to poets who set
the vivid life of city states into history and permanence,
who cast lassos in the air,
        caught ethereal spirits and emotions
floating above the heads of people
in squares of celebration
and set them into the shapes of runes lighting up
when you read them
as you see a sensation you've always felt
but have never had verified
by the reality of a concrete shape.
I pray I leave behind
not just a record of words
but a poetic spark in more souls
than those who know they have such a lightning inside them,
that I hope grows into a fire of minds
fiercely expressing their free identities
and setting lines of future poets aflame
with the responsibility of their art's capacity
for commemoration,
celebration,
reminding,
remembering,
and encapsulating the dynamic realities of this place,
this time.

THE UNDERGROUND CHAMBER

The paradox of any achievement is
that the road there
isn't as brightly lit
        as the finish line;
believe it or not
I never thought my content
  made me a likely candidate
        for something like "Poet Laureate",
the images in my imaginings
aren't attached to patriotism
          without question
          or reassurance
          without awareness,
I'm not engaging in Vitamin C's school nostalgia
or chaining lines together for chain restaurants
because my words don't mix
            with tea or coffee in a cup
            held by two hands at once.
I conjure vain demons and indifferent beasts
              alongside a dark god's dry humour
              and stories of the abyss,
but I think it's a point of Canadian pride
        that David Cronenberg made such a monstrous Fly,
        that Streetsville cultivated
              hellish imagery for Hannibal
and that the winter of '74 in Toronto
      gave birth to (the first) Black Christmas,
in fact,
it was the bone chilling power
of that slasher movie that made me see
how a story can leave you speechless

when I was fifteen and saw it on TV.
The point is
I don't think the city I represent,
is a horror show or a cosmic dystopia,
I do what I do to make it a place
where people can rediscover their singular voice,
        the one fate's path and the status quo file down,
by embracing my strange perspective,
by making spaces where people can be who they are
    in one-on-one conversations,
and by pointing poets towards the doorways
        I thought only opened in dreams
        because too many of those who step through
cover up the passages they use
to preserve egos built on the illusion
that achievements lose value if they inspire
                anyone to fly higher than them.

REFLECTIONS IN A MISSISSAUGA WOODLAND

It's a gradual, organic invasion
taking back altered scenes no one photographed
emerging over broken, bladed machines.

You should leave
and return when this place
occurs to you by chance

if you want
to not only see progress
but also recognize
evidence of its reality.

A web of branches
straining to hold back
crushing, atmospheric noise
carried on sharp winds snaking
in like babbling, gentle waves.

Some stumbling upon the river
find it magnificent,
even mighty,
in the absence of knowing
how the trails and eroded shores where they wander
sat beneath currents flowing
high overhead,
their ecosphere inverted
where what once ruled
still hibernates on the other side.

WHEN I TUNED OUT THE GHOSTLY SINGER

Although
I say
I simply cannot
show sincere belief in some
figurative faith,
I also can't explain why
these strange events took place:
once during a winter's night,
                    on a bridge above a creek
I stared into darkness between trees
                    trying hard to seek
the source of a frosted, ethereal voice
as it accosted my sense of reason
until a nearby lantern went out
                                        with a quiet shriek.
I said nothing and
walked on to the road's
bright electric glow
where my mind sought out
a nightlight somewhere
in-between opaque
                    shadows of the world.

JOURNEYMAN'S GREENBELT

A way through morning mist—
there's a world on the other side
of fences across from
the wild overgrowth into
which so many pilgrims
have disappeared. Some still look back
through dense vines and thick trees.
I see routes branching off and away
but
I'm always wondering what kind of energy
I'll find
If I keep hiking around twisting bends,
running the
gauntlet between destination and memory
over a wide path
that feels like balancing
                    on the edge of a knife.

LAND ACCESSIBLE

Vast mysteries my child mind imagined
in the park like a giant's path, by a creek
behind the street where I lived, in a legend

while playing among trees time and age makes weak,
pretending that this green corridor of ours
leads to magic plains of paper dreams we seek

but then there were only dirt paths, like scars,
for traversing long snaking strands of green space
without street lamps to offer lights like bright stars

until an aware, re-thought plan put in place
a path paved over how the lack of one kept
accessible wheels away from so much grace

BY THE SYNTHETIC PEARL POET

If my memory fades, make me walk the trails,
holding my hand or pushing through this haven
after sitting me still and reading out stories of Sinbad,
not because it'll bring up emotions or birth a recollection,
but so I'll again feel, for the first time,
a child's wonder at not knowing where we are or what lies
farther than the trees, past the flimsy fence,
so I see sacred temples or ancient shrines
in concrete tunnels and a towering, titanic overpass
feeling
imagination shape the reality
of my whole being
in ways that are a scarcity
after maturing.

A TURN OF THE WORLD

A famous song says
Nothing changes on New Year's Day,
not because nothing does
but because change
is constantly spread
over every day, hour, second,
or other way of measuring time you can name;
someone studying
    a book of linguistics
asked me to appreciate our state of flux
by thinking of every noun I know,
       every town, street, or item,
as a type of verb instead,
    so a wooden table
    isn't dead or lifeless;
    when it holds a flickering candle
    it's reborn
from a felled tree's form
    to rise and perform an act
    like Atlas holding up the sky,
although new beginnings
    are best observed
from a still point,
like what I felt on the way
    on paths in Riverwood Park,
    guiding hikes
    through forests and ravines
       along the Credit River

while volunteering for a transition
into the role of a teacher,
like the land's change from private estate
to a space in the city
showing stillness's place
amidst innovation
where tall grass grows
over old farm gear
and the once-empty field by the entrance
becomes a floral terrace…
or former gardens of Babylon
hanging through time's continuum.

SET THE TRUTH ON OUR GROUND

Who are the half-seen figures you see circling the fire on
parliament hill? Who do you see in the flickering light?
We see more heroes than we'll honour
we see more ghosts than we'll admit
as spectral bodies keep circling a centennial flame,
    shadows bound to light,
            waiting for their song.

If you ask how long we'll acknowledge names generations forgot,
first remember the permanence of soil, of histories lost
and the voices echoing from long ago
before I remind you that atonement has no finish line
        or celebration for an ego chasing forgiveness,
        that the act itself and a hope for expanding awareness
        are goals unto themselves,
                                detached from accomplishment
and rooted instead
in a steep responsibility.

Our railroad binding northern lands,
            has both a last spike and a last soul binding it to the earth.
A single national idea dissolves during touch,
reforming around fingers extending towards it,
as it always has:
a healing wisdom risen from the prairies,
morphing faces of the dominion's identity,
our flown symbol's late birth,
the story of an anthem's evolution
                transcending individual words,
                        and pulling us past old laws
                        demanding one eye for another.

Arriving from Portugal, my own grandfather
        worked farmlands
to bring his family across the ocean
to forge lives unthinkable on their island;
                a signed letter sat on his mantle
                from the Prime Minister for a fiftieth
                        anniversary of arrival,
my pride mixing
with a hope that right honourable hands
sign enough letters
for every hand calloused in the country's formation
and everything taken as the nation
landed on Atlantic shores.
Both bright and shadowy mountains of the past loom high;
their silhouettes meeting at a narrowing point
where pride in our past can't exclude its reality
                if we're to keep faith in our future.

HALLOWEEN IS 2020

I can only shrug with high shoulders
when someone says October
means a fearful season is finally here
in this year of our "unprecedented" Lord 2020,

beginning with wildfire,
souls gunned down
or knelt on till death,
and a virus scheming through Summer
before Fall brought news
of a fellow poet imprisoned in British Columbia
for a ceremony on unceded
                    Indigenous land.

Old vintage photos
from Hallows Eve a century past
bring their animal heads and nightmare masks
back to life:
children dispelling terrors
            revealed in dreams
            by becoming their fears,
but it's getting harder
            to create horrors
            that outpace the cruel inventiveness
                            of our present reality.

A million patterns
carved into pumpkin Jack-O-Lanterns
cross the range of human imagination,
though a return to the tradition of using
          Irish

or Cornish turnips
would make a better symbol for the age
with grotesque, frozen faces
        grimacing during a gaunt endurance
                                                    of existence
                                    or the powers that be,
able to scare off more spirits than those appearing
          during Samhain in Somerset
          because we're a misfit collection too,

seeing how
sewing costumes from cultures
          doesn't bring knowledge
like when we embody
the unique corporeal phantoms
     and abstract monstrosities
           keeping us from sleep
while in search of permanent
                                 haunted masks
buried deep.

THE EVOLUTION OF SANTA KLAUS

Two young eyes grew wide
staring out their frosted bedroom window
on Christmas eve,
imagining a jolly, bearded Santa
in a red suit with white fur trim
on a sleigh gliding across heaven,
hitched to mythic reindeer
bonded by song
but those same eyes, now grown bloodshot
hallucinate a vision of Santa Klaus
with a beard,
a mohawk,
and a red suit with white trim cut
from the fur of hunted polar bears:
its sleeves torn off
to show muscular, tattooed arms
as he flies to the driving rhythm
of German industrial metal
blaring from speakers on the sides of his sleigh
(the reindeer pulling it hate each other
but they have no identity
beyond the song that binds them)
while Klaus fires a flamethrower through the night
because he can't carry enough coal
to fill every sinner's stocking
as they lie in bed
so he incinerates their Christmas trees
into lumps of charcoal instead.

MISSISSAUGATOWN

A municipality
with Pearson to welcome the world,
amalgamated villages
                    of small business

suburban streets spawning
theatre directors,
poets,
athletes,
and new musicians,
imagining, planning:
give them a place to play.

It might only be a hope
            or plan right now but
            we'll again skate on ice,
                or asphalt,
            and gather on green turf under the jumbo screen
            by a library whose pages are blueprints for dreams.

They say our borders are wide and I nod, for there
would be no other way to accommodate all
the groups we've brought together here,
in a festival of bread and honey
like a microcosm of the country.

Landing in the seventies,
new arrivals looked and
saw Tomken road trail far off
into farmland dust
while I see a young town grow
beyond itself to the globe.

STATE-SPONSORED ELEGY

As reported
    by town news,
the funeral
couldn't fit
all the mourners who came
        paying respect to the victim,
                lighting vigils outside
    and following the service's
                online stream
where the city's poet
read verses
dedicated to the deceased,
who was killed by police
when loved ones sought aid
                in a psychiatric
                    emergency,
after which
a city lawyer
immediately stood up to state,
officially,
that the Exceptional Examination Squad
found law enforcement
Justified
in their use of violence
and that no charges were laid
            on any officer,
after which
he said,
So sorry for your loss

and sat down
without missing a beat
in a heavy silence
he mistook for general acceptance
of his missive.

ELECTION SPECIAL

If you fall short
in a federal election,
   a provincial one,
or worry that you will,
never fear
for it's its only a hop, skip,
and baby-kissing jump
to change from MP
as in Member of Parliament,
   or MPP of a province,
   to MP
as in Municipal Politician,
especially in areas
with an official aesthetic
of toxic positivity
under a British
         parliamentary system.

THE SKULL OF A LAWYER

Ask not
how they obtained a state of
Positive vibes only!
Ask instead
what they wiped out,
            dragged in a bloody bag to the curb
        or disappeared
so that positivity
could run for office unopposed.

What's more,
look for inferred
worlds between worlds
where an abscess too dense for light
is its own kind of death,
shout into it
and listen for the areas choking off your yell
to find the graves of ingloriously muted voice
and then be sure
to say the prayers they can't when you do.

Now, for the sake of sustainable sanity,
I have to separate
        from believers in the idea
        that *legally required*
        and *ethically correct*
        are synonymous,
who endlessly repeat,
        but it's allowed
        each time
        a wrong act is addressed,

who only want
        a pleasant accountability,
who, at best,
        lose their grasp of reality
        by thinking a cleverly written clause
        can make mustard in coffee
        taste good,
and who, at worst,
        forgo their humanity
        by finding some line
        in some subsection
        more moving than a sick child's
        cry for comfort.

ABOUT THE MISSISSAUGA'S THIRD POET LAUREATE

The Third Poet Laureate of Mississauga served from April 2019 to November 2021. He partook or lead many initiatives such as, but not limited to, running workshops with the Mississauga Library, hosting online events with the Peel Environmental Youth Alliance, hosting the monthly YTGA Open Mic at Studio.89, performing for Mississauga Museums during two Robbie Burns' Day events, leading two "Hike and Write" outdoor workshops at the Riverwood Conservancy, facilitating poetry readings for new poets with the "Outer Haven" series, hosting the city's annual poetry slam, and reciting "In Flanders Fields" at Remembrance Day ceremonies. He recited original poetry at events like the Mayor's New Year's Levee, Councilor Fonseca's Family Fun Skate, Hazel McCallion's 99th Birthday, and Canada Day 2019. He worked with the city and artist Hiba Abdallah to create the "Poetry Lane" public-works installation of original poetry with graphic design along the Burnhamthorpe Trail. He represented Mississauga at Laureate City 2019 by VerseFest at the National Archives in Ottawa.

ACKNOWLEDGMENTS

The following poems first appeared in these publications. The poet acknowledges these organizations with thanks and gratitude:

"The Nervousness Manifesto" (*Hypnopomp Literary Magazine*)

"Like Tears in Ice" (*Drom Arts Collective "Togetherness" Anthology*)

"Psycho-Lycanthropy" (*Former People Journal*)

"Where No Suns Shine" (*Pif Magazine*)

"Speak Friend and Enter" (*Auroras and Blossoms Poetry Journal*)

"Iconoclast Decorating LTD." (*Otherwise Engaged Literary Journal*)

"Take a Balloon and Go Sailing" (*Emerge Literary Journal*)

"Chicken Little in the Style of a 1970's Conspiracy Thriller" (*Former People Journal*)

"I Never Said Thank You" (*Train: A Poetry Journal*)

"The Hate Parade" (*American Diversity Report*)

"Criminological" (*Unlikely Stories Mark V*)

"Post-Secondary Stress Disorder: Know the Symptoms" (*The Misfit Quill*)

"It Rains a Lot in Fifth Dimension" (*The Misfit Quill*)

"We Shall Meditate on the Beaches" (*Otherwise Engaged Literary Journal*)

"Defender of the Absurd" (*Otherwise Engaged Literary Journal*)

"A Mythic Greek Torment" (*Hypnopomp Literary Magazine*)

"Madman Above the City" (*Malfunction Literary Magazine*)

"Fist of the Third Quarter Moon" (*Hypnopomp Literary Magazine*)

"Swinging Swords like Shinobi" (*Hypnopomp Literary Magazine*)

"You Become Something Else Entirely" (*Otherwise Engaged Literary Journal*)

"The Daughter of Oceanus" (*Flora Fiction Literary Magazine*)

"The Rains of Azzirad Fell" (*The Misfit Quill*)

"Tapping a Strained Mind for Syrup" (*Subterranean Blue Poetry*)

"My Mind Stripped Bare by Its Absence, Uneven" (*Unlikely Stories*)

"From Ancient Verse" (yoursauga.com)

"The Underground Chamber" (*Former People Journal*)

"When I Tuned Out the Ghostly Singer", "Journeyman's Greenbelt", "Land Accessible", "By the Synthetic Pearl Poet, Mississauguatown" (From the Poetry Lane Public Works Project in Mississauga)

"Truth on Our Ground" (*Modern Mississauga Media*)

NOTABLE SPOKEN WORD POETRY PERFORMANCES/WORKSHOPS

2024 Performances

- Featured Poet at **Clown House Arts Collective "Spark Up" Chapbook Launch**, Tail of the Junction, Toronto (*January 21*)
- Featured Poet at **Bridging the Border International Open Mic Night**, Studio.89, Mississauga (*March 15*)
- Featured Poet at **VerseDeli**, Krave Coffee, Toronto (*March 28*)
- Featured Poet at **Poetry in Parkdale**, Larry's Folly, Toronto (*April 6*)
- Featured Poet at **Art Bar Poetry Series**, Free Times Cafe, Toronto (*April 22*)
- Guest Reader at **5th Annual Mississauga Poetry Slam**, Living Arts Centre, Mississauga (*April 24*)
- Featured Poet at **Clown House Arts Collective "Angels vs Devils" Chapbook Launch**, Imperial Pub, Toronto (*May 3*)
- Featured Poet at **Liars' Club Comedy Talk Show and Reading Series**, The Epochal Imp, Toronto (*May 29*)
- Featured Poet & Curator at **Tartan Turban Secret Readings #42**, Barrett and Welsh, Toronto (*June 28*)
- Featured Poet at **Exprose Reading Series**, Studio.89, Mississauga (*July 27*)
- Featured Poet at **Bonafide Banter Open Mic Night**, Teddy Beer, Toronto (*September 12*)
- Featured Poet at **Spoken Word Night**, EQF Lounge, Toronto (*September 27*)
- Featured Poet at **The Milk Magazine Reading Series**, Type Books, Toronto (*December 4*)

2023 Performances and Workshops

- Featured Poet at **Poetry Open Mic**, Buddies in Bad Times Theatre, Toronto (*March 19*)
- Featured Poet at **Art Bar Poetry Series**, Free Times Cafe, Toronto (*April 17*)
- Featured Poet at **Aurora Exhibition**, University of Toronto, Mississauga (*April 28*)
- Featured Speaker at **Storystar Storytelling Event**, On-Task Studio, Toronto (*May 18*)
- Featured Poet at **Station Gallery Poetry Open Mic**, Station Gallery, Whitby (*June 7*)
- Featured Poet at **High Park Public Library**, Toronto (*July 6*)
- Featured Poet at **Tartan Turban Secret Readings #39**, Barrett and Welsh, Toronto (*August 8*)
- Facilitator for **A Poetic Story Circle Workshop**, Studio.89, Mississauga (*September 20*)
- Featured Poet at **Liars' Club Reading Series**, The Epochal Imp, Toronto (*November 29*)

ABOUT THE POET

Paul Edward Costa is an award-winning poet, spoken word artist, and teacher who served as Mississauga's 3rd Poet Laureate from April 2019 to November 2021. During his tenure, he led and participated in numerous initiatives, including workshops with the Mississauga Library, outdoor "Hike and Write" sessions at the Riverwood Conservancy, and poetry readings for new poets through the "Outer Haven" series. He also hosted the city's annual poetry slam, recited "In Flanders Fields" at Remembrance Day ceremonies, and performed original poetry at high-profile events such as the Mayor's New Year's Levee, Hazel McCallion's 99th Birthday, and Canada Day 2019. Paul collaborated with artist Hiba Abdallah to create the "Poetry Lane" public art installation along the Burnhamthorpe Trail and represented Mississauga at Laureate City 2019 by VerseFest in Ottawa.

Paul is a full member of the League of Canadian Poets and a former Director of the Art Bar Poetry Series. He has published over 60 poems and stories in journals such as *Poetry Undressed Quarterly*, *Train: A Poetry Journal*, and *Blank Spaces Magazine*. His poetry collection, *The Long Train of Chaos* (Kung Fu Treachery Press), and his flash fiction book, *God Damned Avalon* (Mosaic Press), have both received critical acclaim. As a spoken word artist, Paul has featured at events like Shab-e She'r, Wild Writers, and the Victoria Poetry Project's Tongues of Fire. He has also hosted event series such as the YTGA Open Mic at Studio.89 and Verses Out Loud.

Follow Paul on Twitter, YouTube, Instagram, and Facebook to stay updated on his creative journey.